BASIC CHEMISTRY

SOME BASIC CHEMISTRY CONCEPT

SWATI VITTHALRAO BAGAL

This Book is dedicated to all the students Worldwide.I hope this book is useful for all the students to complete their basic knowledege of Chemistry.Specially those students who have fear about chemistry subject.

Contents

Foreword

Special Thanks to Prof.Mahesh Aher and my family to their endless support.

This book should become the Gold standard of Chemistry in the areas of flexibility,accuracy and connection with its readers .

This is,to the best of my knowledge ,the first and simple basic terms related book .

Preface

This Book is Prepared with the motive that students of the world will be competant enough to meet the challenges of academic and professional courses on national level.

This Book is specially designed for B.Sc.(Hon.) and M.Sc.Students of Indian as well as Foreign Universities.

This book is also very useful for Engineering Students.

Near about all the basic Concept related Physical Chemistry ,Inorganic Chemistry,Organic Chemistry and Analytical Chemistry are covered in this book.

This book is beneficial for students for Orals,Competitive Exams,Practical Exams and for Job Interview .

In this Chemistry Book basic terms are explained in the very simple language.

The Author are sincerely Thankful to Prof.Mahesh Aher for their inspiration and unlimited cooperation during the preparation of the whole book content.

The suggestions towards the further improvement of the book shall be greatfully acknoledged.

I express my sincere thanks to Publishing consultant Miss .Shereen for help me to publishing this book.

SWATI BAGAL

Readers in Chemistry, Subject Matter Expert

Kopargaon.

Acknowledgements

I would like to express my special thanks gratitude to Prof.Mahesh Aher to their great inspiration and support to complete this book

SWATI BAGAL

Subject Matter Expert

Prologue

This book is generally designed for B.Sc (Hons.) and P.G.Students and Engineering of Indian and Forign Universities .

This book Contains near about all Chemistry basic terms which are useful for students for their Exams as well as Interviews.

CHAPTER ONE

Some Basic Concept of Physical Chemistry

CHAPTER TWO

Some Basic Concept of Inorganic Chemistry

CHAPTER THREE

Some Basic Concept of Organic Chemistry

CHAPTER FOUR

Some Basic Concept Of Analytical Chemistry

I hope this book is useful for students .

www.ingramcontent.com/pod-product-compliance
Ingram Content Group UK Ltd.
Pitfield, Milton Keynes, MK11 3LW, UK
UKHW061828190726
13853UKWH00009B/2497

9 798887 838861